COPYRIGHT PAGE

Copyright © 2019 by V. Anand
All rights reserved. No part of this publication may be reproduced, distributed, or transmitted in any form or by any means, including photocopying, recording, or other electronic or mechanical methods, without the prior written permission of the publisher, except in the case of brief quotations embodied in critical reviews and certain other noncommercial uses permitted by copyright law.

TABLE OF CONTENTS

CHAPTER 1:
Introduction to IoT　　　　　　　　　　　　　　　3

CHAPTER 2:
IOT Communications & Standards and Regulations　　11

CHAPTER 3:
The 3GPP Connectivity Family　　　　　　　　　　20

CHAPTER 4:
Data, Platforms and Privacy　　　　　　　　　　　30

CHAPTER 5:
Markets and Business Models　　　　　　　　　　　41

CHAPTER 6:
Selected Case Studies　　　　　　　　　　　　　　51

CHAPTER 1

INTRODUCTION TO IOT

- Debugging the IoT
- Today's IoT Challenges
- IoT Recommendations
- Business Case of IoT
- IoT Application

WHAT IS IOT?

Internet of Things (IoT) is the Combination

- Devices
- Vehicles
- Buildings and other
- Products items embedded with
    - Electronics
    - Software
    - Sensors
    - Network connectivity
    - Objects to collect and exchange data.

VARIOUS NAMES, ONE CONCEPT

- M2M (Machine to Machine)
- "Internet of Everything" (Cisco Systems)
- "World Size Web" (Bruce Schneier)
- "Skynet" (Terminator movie)

IOT IMPLEMENTATION CONCEPTS
IoT implementations is

- Is approach based
- The complex nature of each project
- As disparate components of the ecosystem of IoT.

SENSORS

Sensor is an electronic device providing

- Electrical
- Optical
- Digital data

Then derived from a physical condition or event.

- The Data produced from the sensors is then

Transformed with another device
- Output which is useful in decision making

Selection Process for devices
- Purpose (Temperature, Motion)
- Accuracy
- Reliability
- Range
- Resolution
- Intelligent level
- Sensors which are cheaper
- IoT Sensors

CHALLENGES:
- Power
- Device Security
- Device to Device Interoperability

NETWORKS
It is defined as Transmission of the signals

- Collected by the networks
- By different components whihc includes routers, bridges

Will help in Transformation of combining with technlogies such as

- Wi-Fi, Bluetooth,

How Will 5G Help IOT Transformation

- Low Power Wi-Fi,
- Wi-Max,
- Ethernet
- Long Term Evolution (LTE)
- Li-Fi

Driving Forces are below

- Virtualization
- XaaS
- IPv6

Challenges facing network implementation in IoT:

- Increase in Connected devices
- Availability of networks coverage
- Security Layer
- Power consumption

Business Case of IoT

- Transformational
    - IoT can help
    - Build better relationships with your customers,
    - Boost productivity
    - Unlock new revenue streams.
    - Can benefit your organization using Innovation

Business Case of IoT

- It is very much required now to challenge the competition
    - Focus on the risks associated with IoT
        - ROI, complexity, privacy and security.
    - Need a plan for issues, mitigate risk, and plan for a successful IoT project.

Business Case of IoT

- Be always Ready
    - Practical implementation of Technology
    - We need to define use cases aligned to business complications

CHAPTER 2

IOT COMMUNICATIONS & STANDARDS AND REGULATIONS

- Regulation and Trends
- Basics in Wireless Communications
- IoT Tech Overview
- Pros & Cons of Wireless IoT Technologies
- Wireless Short-Range Technologies
- Low-Power Wider Area Network Technologies
- Overview of Cellular IoT Technologies

STANDARDS

Three types of standards

- Technology -network protocols, communication protocols
- Data-aggregation standards
- Regulatory - Security and privacy of data

US FEDERAL TRADE COMMISSION'S PRIVACY AND SECURITY RECOMMENDATIONS DUBBED THE FAIR INFORMATION PRACTICE PRINCIPLES

- Choice and notice:
  - Users can chose and also enterprise should notify users when their personal information is being recorded.
  - For all IoT applications that aggregate information
- Purpose specification and use limitation:
  - Must clearly state the purpose for the collection of those data.
  - Data usage should be having a purpose specified

US FEDERAL TRADE COMMISSION'S PRIVACY AND SECURITY RECOMMENDATIONS DUBBED THE FAIR INFORMATION PRACTICE PRINCIPLES

Data minimization:

- Company has the right to collect data for a specific purpose
- Delete that data after the intended use.
- Restricts the scope of analysis
- Slicing and dicing the IoT data.

Security and accountability:

- Collect and store data are accountable
- Deploy security systems
  - Unauthorized access, modification, deletion, or use of the data.

TECHNOLOGY STANDARDS

Network protocols:
- A set of rules by which machines
- Identify and authorize each other.
- Interoperability issues result from multiple network protocols

Communication protocols:
- Devices are connected to a network
- They identify each other through communication protocols
- Various communication protocols are used for device-to-device

Components of IOT Implementation
- Implementing is not easy as the components of the ecosystem of IoT.

Data aggregation standards:
- Data collected from multiple devices
- Different formats and at different sampling rates
- Transformation includes
  - Splitting, merging, sorting
- Ttransforming the data into a desire format
- Loading is loading the data into a database for analytics applications.

WIRELESS COMMUNICATION TECHNOLOGIES

Definition
- Any communication device or application.
- Bluetooth to Wi-Fi LANs and MANs, satellite communication,
- Wide spread applications
  - Video conferencing
  - Telemedicine
  - Distance learning, and much more

THE WIRELESS TECHNOLOGIES

Types of wireless technologies

- Wireless LANs (WiFi)
  - 802.11 standards
  - Mobility support
- Wireless MANs (WiMaX)
  - 802.16 standard

Wireless v/s Wired networks

- Regulations of frequencies
  - Limited availability
  - Useful frequencies are occupied
- Bandwidth and delays
  - Low transmission rates
    - Few Kbits/s to some Mbit/s.

Higher delays

- Several hundred milliseconds
  - Higher loss rates
    - Susceptible to interference, e.g., engines, lightning
- Always shared medium
  - Lower security
  - Radio interface easy access

Technologies

- Bluetooth
- GSM
- GPRS
- CDMA
- Wi-Fi

CDMA

- Code Division Multiple Access.
- Uses spread spectrum techniques.
- Data is sent in small packets and are discrete frequencies.
- Unique spreading code.
- Greatest advantage- doesn't assign a single frequency to user.
- Secured transmission.

BlueTooth

- It is defined as a wireless technology for exchanging data over short distances.
    - Any data or information can be transmitted faster and with a high speed.
- Using short-wavelength - ISM band
    - 2.4 to 2.485 GHz.
- The IEEE standardized Bluetooth as IEEE 802.15.1.

GPRS

What is GPRS?

- General Packet Radio Service is a packet based wireless communication service
- Permits data rates from 56 kbps and 114 kbps
- Continuous connection with the Internet for mobile phone and computer users.

WiFi

- Wi-Fi (Wireless Fidelity) to IEEE 802.11 standard for Wireless Local Area Networks (WLANs).
- Wi-Fi Network - connect computers to the internet and to the wired network.

How Will 5G Help IOT Transformation

GSM

- Stands for Global System For Mobile Communication
- It is a digital mobile telephony system
- First generation cellular replacement

IoT ecosystem and Connectivity Cellular technologies enable a wide range of IoT services

IoT ecosystem and Connectivity

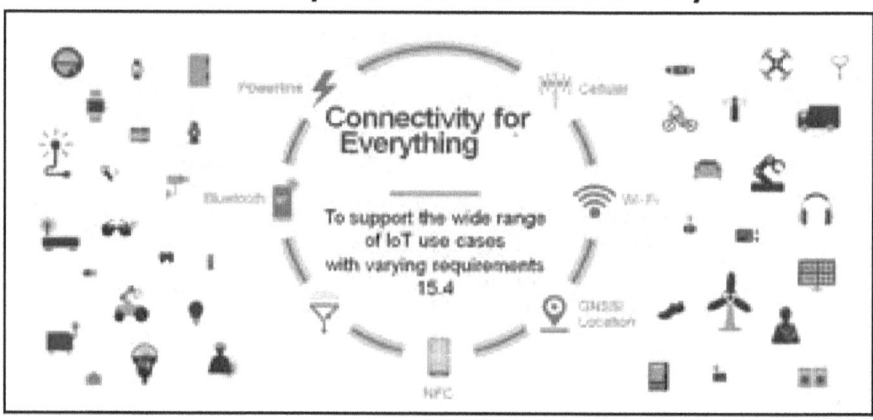

Cellular technologies enable a wide range of IoT services

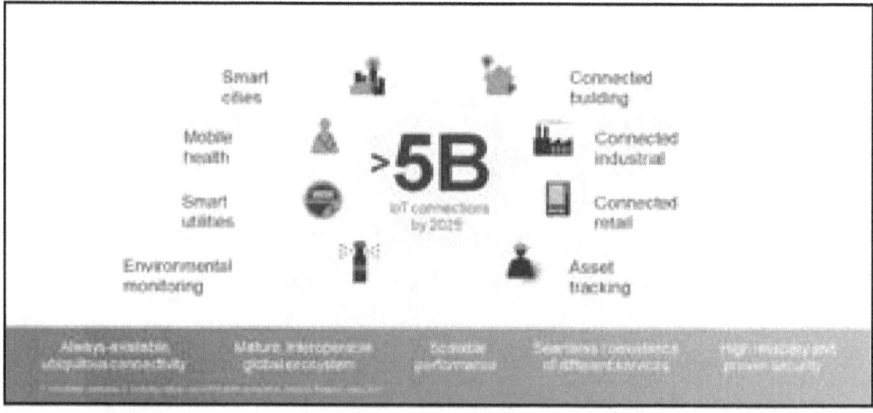

Why LPWAN Technologies?

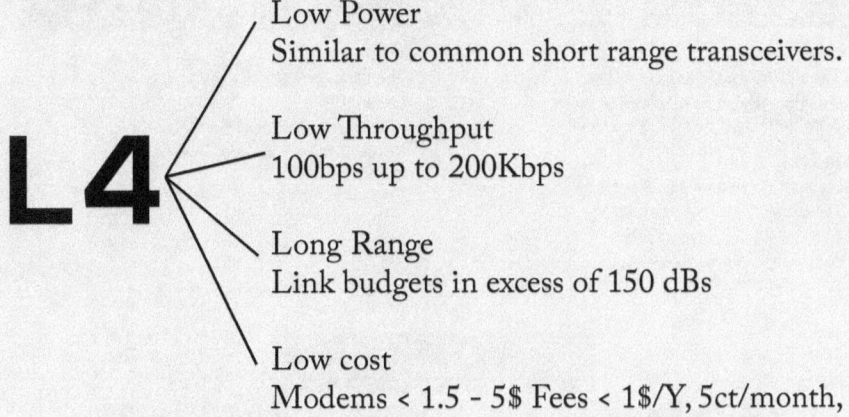

L4
- Low Power
  Similar to common short range transceivers.
- Low Throughput
  100bps up to 200Kbps
- Long Range
  Link budgets in excess of 150 dBs
- Low cost
  Modems < 1.5 - 5$ Fees < 1$/Y, 5ct/month,

LPWAN Technologies role in The IoT Ecosystem

- LPWAN technologies will generate close to $ 3B only in the
- LPWAN module business by 2023
- Three technologies (LoRa, SigFox, NB_IoT) will concentrate
- 90% LPWAN technologies in the market by 2023.
- Stands for Global System For Mobile Communication
- It is a digital mobile telephony system

Wireless Technology Comparison

	PANs	WLANs	Legacy Cellular	LPWA
Data Rates (messaging, IP data)	Low	Med	High	Low
Cost (and complexity)	Low	Med/Low	High	Low
Current (power consumption)	Low	Med	High	Low
Coverage (range, penetration)	Short	Short	Med	V. Long
User Setup/Install (pairing, connected req.?)	Hard	Hard	Easy	Easy

How Will 5G Help IOT Transformation

LPWA technology snapshot

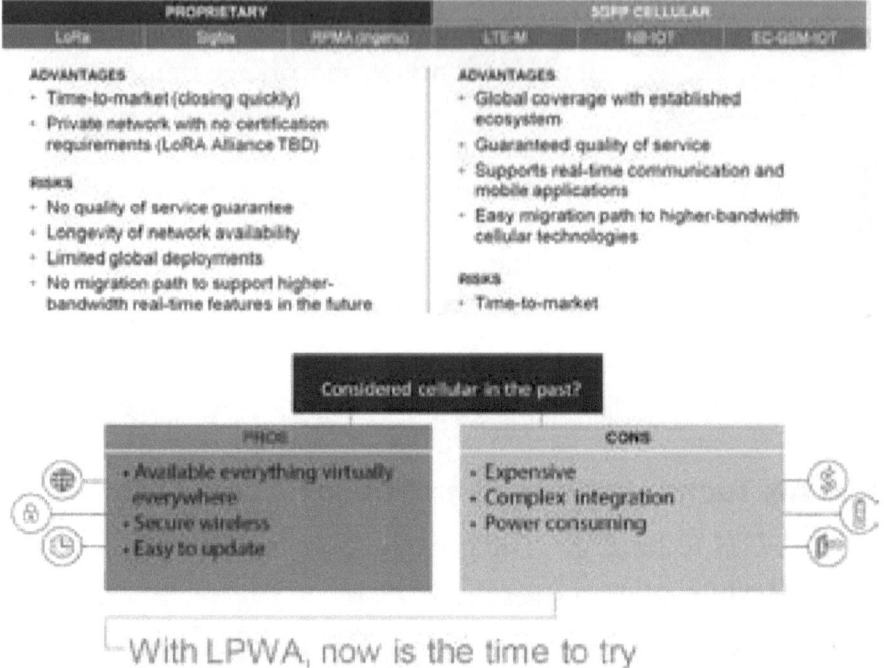

With LPWA, now is the time to try cellular

What makes LPWA a new category of cellular?

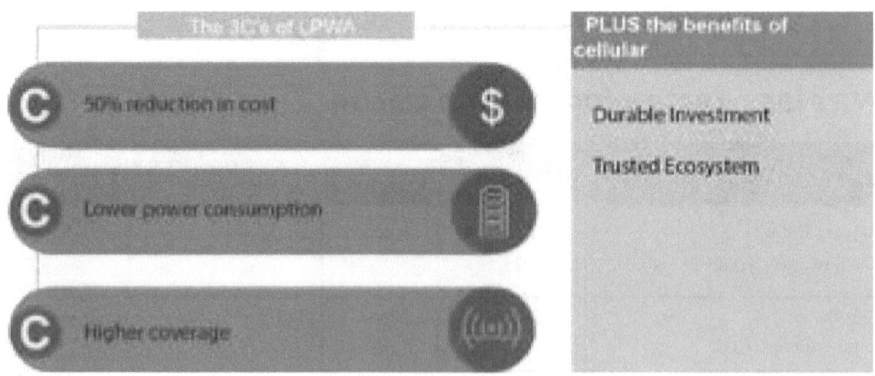

How Will 5G Help IOT Transformation

Comparing low-bandwidth cellular technologies

	NB-IoT		LTE-M		CAT-1
	REL 13	REL 14	REL 13	REL 14	comparison
Current (idle mode)	<15 uA (80s eDRX)				1-2mA (DRX)
Coverage extension	164dB MCL				144 MCL
Cost (future)	<$10				<$15
Worldwide SKU	yes				no
Data Rate (DL/UL)	CAT-NB1 27/65 kbps	CAT-NB2 65/145 kbps	CAT-M1 300/375 kbps	CAT-M1 590/1000 kbps	10/5Mbps
Resource allocation	pre-allocated	~dynamic	dynamic		dynamic
Quality of Service (QoS)	no		yes		yes
Mobility	no		yes		yes
Real Time	no		yes		yes
Voice	no		yes (2018)	Enhanced	yes
Network positioning	no	yes	yes	Enhanced	yes
Network Requirements	mostly software upgrade		software upgrade		minor change

Why LPWAN Technologies?

- Solution □ Filling up the Technology gap

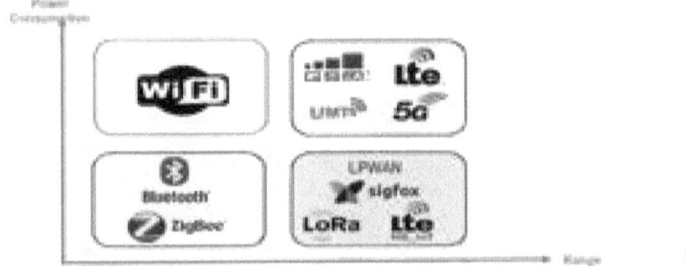

How Will 5G Help IOT Transformation

CHAPTER 3

THE 3GPP CONNECTIVITY FAMILY

- Introduction to 3GPP
- IoT in 3GPP
- EC-GSM
- LTE-M
- NB-IoT
- 3GPP System Design
  - Tech Comparison

LPWA TECHNOLOGY SNAPSHOT

Partnership

Organizational Partners (SDOs)

- Regional standards organizations:
  - ARIB (Japan),
  - ATIS (USA),
  - CCSA (China),
  - ETSI (Europe),
  - TTA (Korea),
  - TTC (Japan),
  - TSDSI (India)

Market Representative Partners

- 16 Market partners representing the broader industry:
  - 5G Americas,
  - COAI (India),
  - CTIA,
  - GCF,
  - GSA,
  - GSMA,
  - IPV6 Forum,
  - MDG (formerly CDG),
  - NGMN Alliance,
  - Small Cell Forum,
  - TCCA,
  - TD Industry Alliance,
  - TD-Forum

NEW:
- Wireless Broadband Alliance
- 5G Infrastructure Association
- Public Safety Communication Europe
- (PSCE) Forum

THE 3GPP ECO-SYSTEM

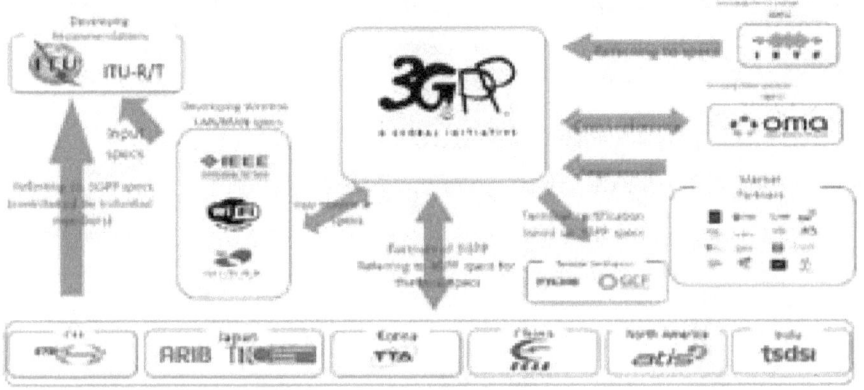

3GPP FACTS AND FIGURES

- ~400 Companies from 39 Countries
- 50.000 delegate days per year
- 40.000 documents per year
- 1.200 specs per Release
- New Release every ~18 months

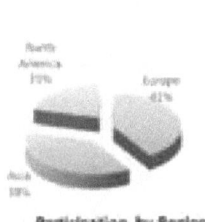

Participation by Region

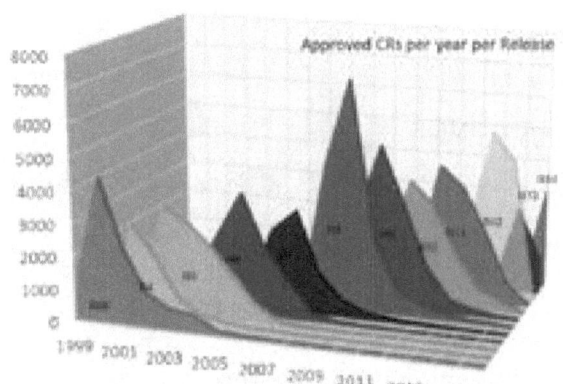

How Will 5G Help IOT Transformation

INTRODUCTION & TIMELINE

- I3GPP – Release 13 is addressing the IoT market
- 3 GPP Portfolio of technologies
  - eMTC - Release-12
  - NB-IoT - For the lower end of the market
  - EC-GSM-IoT
    - EGPRS enhancements with PSM
    - GSM/EDGE markets prepared for IoT
- Release 14 is under Planning

INTRODUCTION & TIMELINE

	eMTC (LTE Cat M1)	NB-IoT	EC-GSM-IoT
Deployment	In-Band LTE	In-band & Guard-band LTE, standalone	In-band GSM
Coverage*	155.7 dB	164 dB for standalone, 154 others	164 dB, with 33dBm power class; 154 dB, with 23dBm power class
Downlink	OFDMA, 15 KHz tone spacing, Turbo Code, 16-QAM, 1 Rx	OFDMA, 15 KHz tone spacing, 1 Rx	TDMA/FDMA, GMSK and 8PSK (optional), 1 Rx
Uplink	SC-FDMA, 15 KHz tone spacing, Turbo code, 16 QAM	Single tone, 15 KHz and 3.75 KHz spacing; SC-FDMA, 15 KHz tone spacing, Turbo code	TDMA/FDMA, GMSK and 8PSK (optional)
Bandwidth	1.08 MHz	180 KHz	200KHz per channel. Typical system bandwidth of 2.4MHz (smaller bandwidth down to 600 KHz being studied within Rel-13)
Peak rate (DL/UL)	1 Mbps for DL and UL	DL: ~50 Kbps; UL: ~50 for multi-tone, ~20 Kbps for single tone	For DL and UL (using 4 timeslots): ~70 kbps (GMSK), ~240kbps (8PSK)
Duplexing	FD & HD (type B), FDD & TDD	HD (type B), FDD	HD, FDD
Power saving	PSM, ext. I-DRX, C-DRX	PSM, ext. I-DRX, C-DRX	PSM, ext. I-DRX
Power class	23 dBm, 20 dBm	23 dBm, others TBD	33 dBm, 23 dBm

EMTC

Objectives

- Long battery life: ~10 years of operation
- Low device cost:
- Extended coverage: >155.7 dB
- Variable rates: ~10 kbps to 1 Mbps

Deployment
- Can be deployed in any LTE spectrum
- Coexist with other LTE services within the same bandwidth
- Support FDD, TDD and half duplex (HD) modes
- Reuse existing LTE base stations with software update

Main PHY/RF features
- Narrowband operation - 1.08 MHz bandwidth
- Frequency - narrowband for frequency diversity
- TTI bundling/repetition to achieve large coverage enhancements
- New UE power class of 20 dBm
- Further cost reduction beyond Cat 0

REL-14: EMTC ENHANCEMENTS

Main feature enhancements
- Support for positioning (E-CID and OTDOA)
- Support for Multicast (SC-PTM)
- Mobility for inter-frequency measurements
- Higher data rates
    - Specify HARQ-ACK bundling in CE mode A in HD-FDD
    - Larger maximum TBS
    - Larger max. PDSCH/PUSCH channel bandwidth
    - In CE mode A
    - Voice and audio streaming
    - Up to 10 DL HARQ processes
- Support for VoLTE

NB-IOT

Objectives
- Cost Lesser than eMTC
- Extended coverage: 164 dB maximum
- Long battery life:

Main simplification
- Reduced data rate/bandwidth
  - Mobility support
- Protocol optimizations

NB-IoT – Support – Operation:
- Stand-alone
- Guard band
  - Utilizing the unused resource blocks
  - LTE carrier's guard-band
- In-band:
  - Resource blocks -normal LTE carrier

Main PHY features
- Band support - 180 kHz
- Two modes – Uplink support
  - Single tone - 15 kHz- 3.75 kHz tone spacing
  - Multiple tones - 15 kHz tone spacing
- Turbo Code – No downlink Support
- Single transmission mode
  - SFBC with PBCH, PDSCH, PDCCH

- Narrowband channels below:
  - NPSS, NSSS, NPBCH
  - NPDCCH, NPDSCH, NPUSCH, NPRACH

Main radio protocol features

- Single HARQ
- RLC AM mode having status reporting
- PDCP options – 2 below:
  - SRB 0 and 1 only.
  - NAS security
  - PDCP operation – Transparent
  - SRB 0, 1, 2 and one DRB.
  - AS security - RRC connection
- Reduction in broadcast system information

REL-14: NB-IOT ENHANCEMENTS

- Support for OTDOA
  - NB-IoT Rel-13
  - LTE CRS/PRS in 1 PRB
- UTDOA Support for the below use cases:
  - Existing NB-IoT transmission
  - Rel-13 UEs
- Signal with positioning will have
  - SC-PTM Support
    - Less Power consumption
    - Latency reduction
  - Non- Anchor PRB features enhanced
  - Mobility and service continuity enhanced
  - New Power Class inclusion

DRX FOR NB-IOT AND EMTC

C-DRX -I-DRX Modulation

- Connected Mode -C-eDRX

    - DRX cycles extension - 5.12s / 10.24

- Idle mode- I-eDRX
    - DRX cycles -44min eMTC

    - DRX cycles - 3hr for NB-IoT

UPPER LAYER FEATURES

- NB-IOT
- EMTC

UE and Network negotiate for NAS/core network optimization

- Transmission for core network selection
- Changes in procedure needs approval

DIFFERENT DATA TRANSFER OPTIMIZATION – NB-IoT and eMTC:

- CP optimization
    - For Small data with NAS using NAS PDUs encryption
    - RoHC Header Compression using IP PDN connection
    -Re- Architecture

    - MME, S-GW and P-GW combines as one -. C-SG
- UP optimization
    - User plane with RAN
    - Cashing in idle machines
    - Enable connection suspension/resumption on radio/S1 interface

- New features
    - Non-IP data Support
    - IP PDN via P-GW
    - Non-IP via SCEF
    -- SMS transfer
    - Storage and usage of coverage in MME for repititions

EC-GSM-IOT

Objectives

- Long battery life:
- Device cost less with GPRS/GSM
- Extended coverage:
    - 164 dB MCL for 33 dBm UE,
    - 154 dB MCL for 23 dBm UE
- Variable rates:
    - GMSK: ~350bps to 70kbps
    - 8PSK: up to 240 kbps
- 50000 Devices per cell support
- Security Enhanced w.r.t GSM/EDGE

Features

- Logical channels - Coverage
    - Repetitions to support 164 dB MCL
- CDMA increased cell capacity
    - For EC-PDTCH and EC-PACCH

Miscellaneous Features

- DRX Extension -52 min
- System information Optimization
- Idle mode behavior Flexibility

- 2G security Upgrade
  - Integrity protection
  - Mutual authentication
  - Stronger ciphering algorithms
- NAS timer extensions

For very low data rate
  - Extended coverage

- Storing and coverage level usage in SGSN to
  - Unnecessary repetitions

RELEASE -14: EC-GSM-IOT ENHANCEMENTS

Objective:

- Specifying radio interface enhancements -- EC-GSM-IoT
- Alternative mappings to blind physical layer transmissions
  - higher coverage class - EC-PDTCH/EC-PACCH
- MCL improvements
  - 3 dB for low power devices
- Support for positioning

CHAPTER 4

DATA, PLATFORMS AND PRIVACY

- IoT Big Data

- Service Architectures

- IoT Data Platforms

- E-to-E Security

- Privacy and Trust

- EU Data Protection

- IoT Data Forecast

How Will 5G Help IOT Transformation

BIG DATA IN IOT

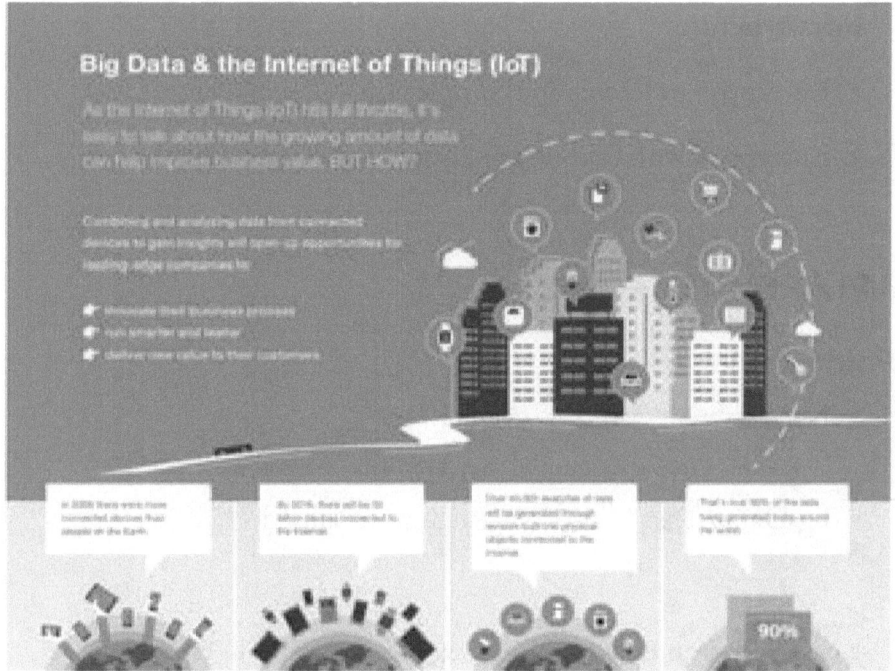

KEY CHALLENGES FOR BUILDING AN IOT APPLICATION

Connect: What can be done to collect data from Intelligent Devices?

- Abstract complexity for every device connectivity
- Standardized integration
    - Multiple devices with enterprise

Analyze: What is the procedures to Data Analysis?

- Reduce noise
    -Detecting business event at real-time
- Big-data analysis

How Will 5G Help IOT Transformation

Integrate: Integrate Data and Synchronization with Event infrastructure

- Enterprise processes IoT simple
- Enterprise with mobile applications to control devices

API ARCHITEC-TURE-

Pointers

- Need to treat events as events!
  - Reason - Infrastructures for handling lots of events are available!
- Big Data / Fast Data infrastructures required

Use case/requirements for choosing the right architecture!

- Existing backend architecture handles the new IoT load?
- Handle huge amount of events in "real-time"?
- Need to do exploratory data analysis? – Filter the data
- Use predictive analytics if necessary
- Network bandwidth between device/gateway and cloud/backend?
- Centralized Vs Decentralized IoT solution?

IoT – Big Data – Open Source Architecture
SECURITY MODEL

IoT Devices Security

- No proper secure storage
- No good processing power for PKI
- No security patches

WHAT IS GDPR?

- Regulation for the treatment of personal data in Europe,
- May 25th 2018 Roll out
- All EU citizen – Personal Data

Who has to comply: Any company processing EU citizens data.

WHAT IS PERSONAL DATA

- Personal data' means any information relating to identifiable natural person ('data subject')
- Reference as name an identification number, location data, an online identifier or to all factors specific to the physical, physiological, genetic, mental, economic, cultural or social identity of that natural person

IoT data is personal Data

- All have to be careful

GDPR – KEY DEFINITIONS

Data Subject: The person whom data are collected and processed for the provisioning of a service

Data Controller: Sets the purpose of the processing (either collected directly or acquired from other sources)

Data Processor: Processes the data for the purpose of providing a service. Might be the same as the Controller

DATA THE NEW OIL - THE OPPORTUNITY

- Digital transformation is being used by every organization
- Data uses:
- Ne Artificial Intelligence and Machine Learning algorithms

- Personalised services
  - Attract new customers

GDPR: TRANSPARENCY

Article 12-14 – What is Information notice ?

Concise, transparent, intelligible, Easily accessible, clear and in plain language

- Should avoid information fatigue
- Name the recipients of personal data
- Keep up-to-date

GDPR: ACCOUNTABILITY

Article 4 and 7 – What is Consent ?

Consent would not legitimize collection of data which is not necessary in relation…

Any freely given, specific, informed and unambiguous indication of the data subject's wishes

By which he or she, by a statement or by a clear affirmative action, signifies agreement to the processing of personal data relating to him or her"

CONSENT KEY REQUIREMENTS

- Cannot share the data or Freely giving the data

Specific Data with consent

- For different data and purpose,

Informed

- An unambiguous indication of wishes

- No pre-ticked boxes, no opt-out

Explicit Consent

- Sensitive data

Should have Proof of consent and possibility to remove

MANAGE CONSENT: IOT SOLUTIONS PERSPECTIVE

Key IoT Challenges

- How to obtain consent through IoT device from Data subject?

- How to remove consent through IoT device of Personal Identifiable Information?

- How to keep the consent updated for many years?

- E.g. triggering new sensors, collecting new data

- How to obtain consent in shared space? Or for shared devices? (cars, home assistants)

GDPR: RIGHT TO PRIVACY

Article 17-19

The right to be informed

- Provide information notice

The right of access

- Free of charge, within a month

The right to rectification

- Within one (or two months)

The right to erasure

- Some exceptions are possible

The right to restrict processing

How Will 5G Help IOT Transformation

- *Retain information but stop processing*

The right to data portability

- *Free of charge, within a month, no hindrance*

The right to object

Marketing and research unless legal basis

Rights in relation to automated decision making and profiling.

IOT CHALLENGES

- Need to know all the collected data from various sensors

- Be able to link data from different data sources with good faith

- Track who you shared the data with – including third party

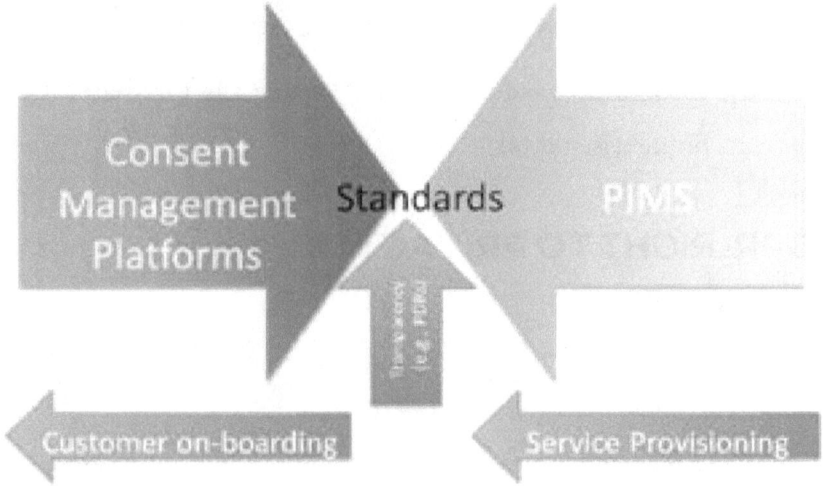

processor

- Track and keep up to date retention period as per the recommended timelines

- Interoperable, machine-readable formats – Storage of data

THE RISKS FOR IOT

How Will 5G Help IOT Transformation

- Key to Understand which data is personal
- Profiling the customers
- Combining data for various purpose
- Data Source and is it with Consen
- Any risk of de-anonymization?

HOW TO BUILD DIGITAL TRUST

- Transparency (Article 12-14, Information notice)
- Accountability (Article 4 and 7, Consent)
- Level of Control (Article 17-19, Data erasure and portability)
    - Measureable properties with Trust

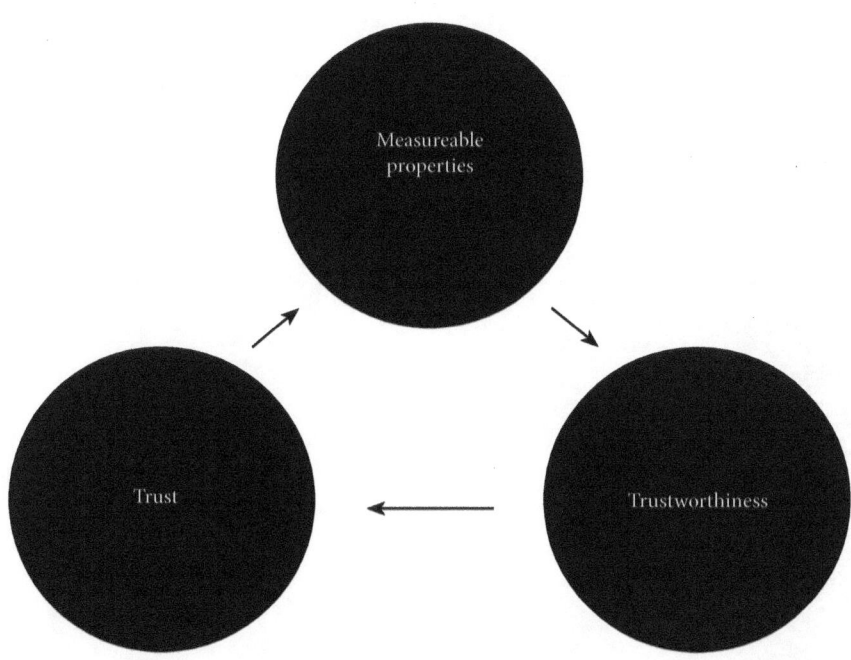

How Will 5G Help IOT Transformation

CHAPTER 5

MARKETS AND BUSINESS MODELS

- Market Overview

- Application Deep-Dive

- Business Models

- IoT Entrepreneurship

How Will 5G Help IOT Transformation

5G AND IOT - MARKET

- 5G is already here and will transform businesses with high speed networks required for IOT business.

- Industrial IoT and 5G market is estimated to grow at a CAGR of +20 % during the forecast period till 2024

5G IOT MARKET DYNAMICS

- 5G networks becomes Commercially viable in 2019 and 2020
    - This will enhance the next generation cellular solutions

- 5G-supported hardware is getting rolled out
    - Companies will use 5G to support their business

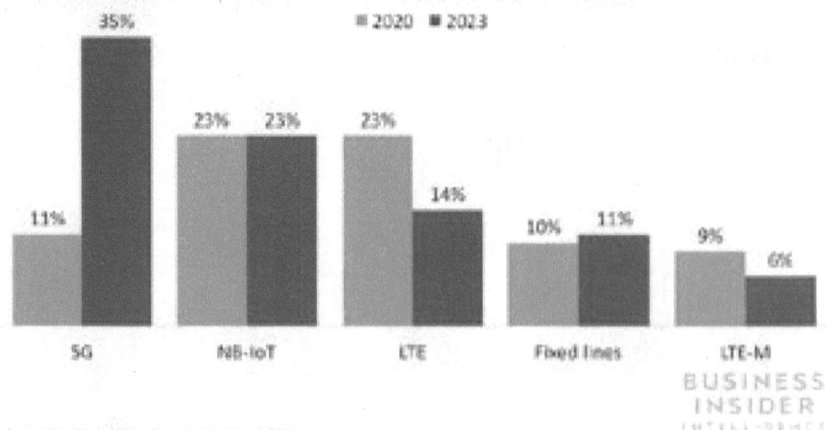

5G AND IOT - MARKET

Companies using IoT devices and the providers of IoT based services and solutions have to be discerning in their determinations of where 5G will help.

5G AND IOT - MARKET -KEY TAKEAWAYS

- 5G will enable new IOT use cases,
    - Real-time monitoring and analytics
    - Remote execution of mission-critical services.

- 5G will offer new capabilities for companies

- Companies with IoT solutions have to harness 5G infrastructure

IOT ENTREPRENEURSHIP

- 5G will build on next generation's solutions as companies are enhancing their investments.

- In the world of IoT, many businesses are supporting modules, sensors, and connectivity and delivery platforms.

- 5G wave is creating new levels of creativity,
    - New use case execution
    - Accelerate the digital transformation 4.0
    - Business reinventing to adapt to the changing trend

- The real benefits of 5G, will be realized after 12 -18 months of commercial launch

- IoT will supercharge everyone's expectation imagination
    - Will be able to create many Unicorns

How Will 5G Help IOT Transformation

CHAPTER 6

SELECTED CASE STUDIES

- B2C vs B2B

- Smart Parking

- Smart Infrastructures

- Smart Fields

How Will 5G Help IOT Transformation

SMART HOMES

- Smart homes are connected products and makes our daily lives- easier, convenient and comfortable.

- The total amount of funding for Smart Home start-ups is more than $2.5bn.

- Few good start up names such as Nest as well as a number of multinational corporations like Philips, Haier, or Belkin.

WEARABLES

- Real fast moving area in IoT.
- Most of them connected with Smart phones.

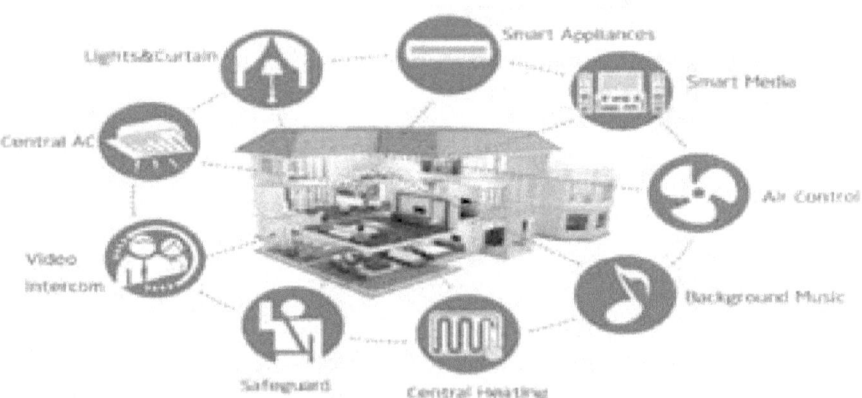

- Devices worn on wrist
- Ex.Smart Watches-SAMSUNG GEAR
- Devices put on like a spectacle
- Ex. Google Glass
- Smart garments.
- Skin coloured Tatoo/patch like sensors.

How Will 5G Help IOT Transformation

SMART CITY

- Smart city includes
    - Traffic management
    - Water distribution
    - Waste management
    - Urban security

- IoT solutions in the area of Smart City solve
    - Traffic congestion
    - Reduce noise and pollution and help make cities safer.

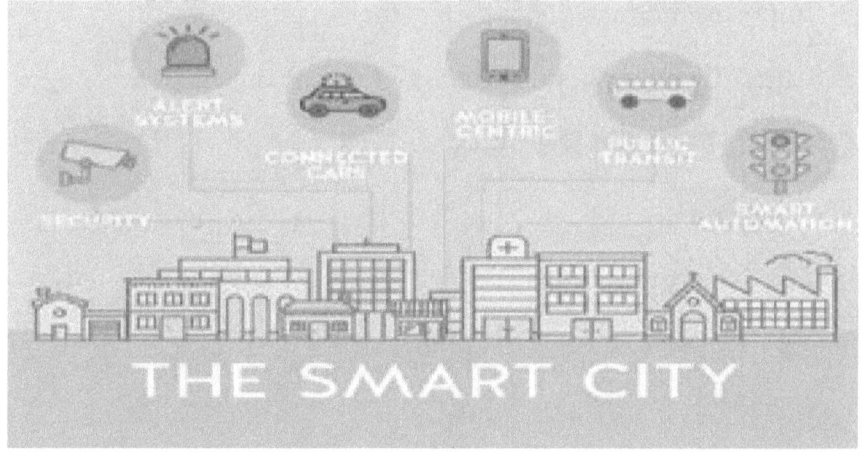

How Will 5G Help IOT Transformation

SMART GRIDS

- Smart grid uses information
  - Behaviors of electricity suppliers
  - Consumers in an automated fashion.

- Useful for
  - Delivery power more efficiently
  - Improve operations
  - Reduce emissions and management costs
  - Restore power failures faster. .

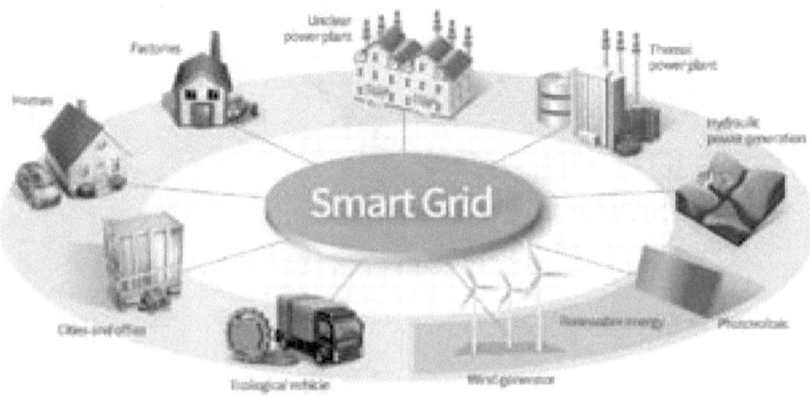

INDUSTRIAL IOT

- Improves productivity and efficiency in businesses.

- Currently not as popular like smart home or wearable

CONNECTED CARS

Two categories:

- In vehicle applications

- V2V (Vehicle to vehicle) applications

How Will 5G Help IOT Transformation

CONNECTED HEALTH

- Everyday monitoring of health indices

SMART RETAIL

- Improving the customer experience

  Optimizing supply chain operation

SMART SUPPLY CHAIN

- Helps in Real time inventory control

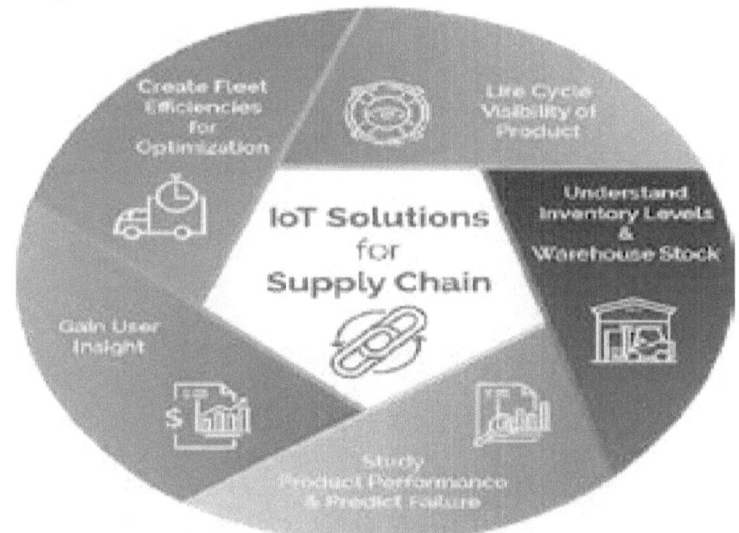

How Will 5G Help IOT Transformation

SMART FARMING

CONCLUSION

5G is expected to provide:

- Faster speeds network speeds as high as 10Gbps

- Lowered latency

- Network support for massive increases in data traffic

- Expansion of cell sites

- Enabling completely new applications
  - Benefits to many IoT application
  - 5G platform will impact many industries including automotive, entertainment, agriculture, manufacturing and IT.

- Wide range of applications will benefit from 5G's ultra-fast networks and real-time responsiveness, such as:
  - Massive Machine Type Communications (mMTC) such as solar-powered streetlights or other Innovations to help citywide infrastructure
  - Device-to-device public safety communications that don't need active cellular coverage
  - Real-time operations employing robotics to link
  - Surgeons with remote site

www.ingramcontent.com/pod-product-compliance
Lightning Source LLC
Chambersburg PA
CBHW030736180526
45157CB00008BA/3187